j 530.8 M663h
Minden, Cecilia
How tall? How wide?

WITHDRAWN

JAN 04 2012

D0432226

21st Century
Basic Skills
Library

HOW TALL?
HOW WIDE?

by Cecilia Minden, PhD

Cherry Lake Publishing • Ann Arbor, Michigan

CHERRY
LAKE
Publishing

Published in the United States of America
by Cherry Lake Publishing
Ann Arbor, Michigan
www.cherrylakepublishing.com

Photo Credits: Cover and page 1, ©Denise Mondloch; pages 3 and 12,
©StudioSmart/Shutterstock, Inc.; pages 4, 6, 10, 12, and 16, ©eskay/
Shutterstock, Inc.; page 8, ©Marcus Miranda/Shutterstock, Inc.; page 10,
©vadim kozlovsky/Shutterstock, Inc.; page 14, ©iStockphoto.com/
Rainbowphoto; page 16, ©RTimages/Shutterstock, Inc.; page 18, ©Steve
Lovegrove/Shutterstock, Inc.; page 20, ©Blue Jean Images/Alamy

Copyright ©2011 by Cherry Lake Publishing
All rights reserved. No part of this book may be reproduced or utilized in
any form or by any means without written permission from the publisher.

Library of Congress Cataloging-in-Publication Data
Minden, Cecilia.
  How tall? How wide?/by Cecilia Minden.
    p. cm.—(21st century basic skills library. Level 1)
  Includes bibliographical references and index.
  ISBN-13: 978-1-60279-848-9 (lib. bdg.)
  ISBN-10: 1-60279-848-6 (lib. bdg.)
  1. Measurement—Juvenile literature. I. Title. II. Series.
  QA465.M55 2010
  530.8'13—dc22   2009048567

Cherry Lake Publishing would like to acknowledge
the work of The Partnership for 21st Century Skills.
Please visit www.21stcenturyskills.org for more information.

Printed in the United States of America
Corporate Graphics Inc.
July 2010
CLFA07

TABLE OF CONTENTS

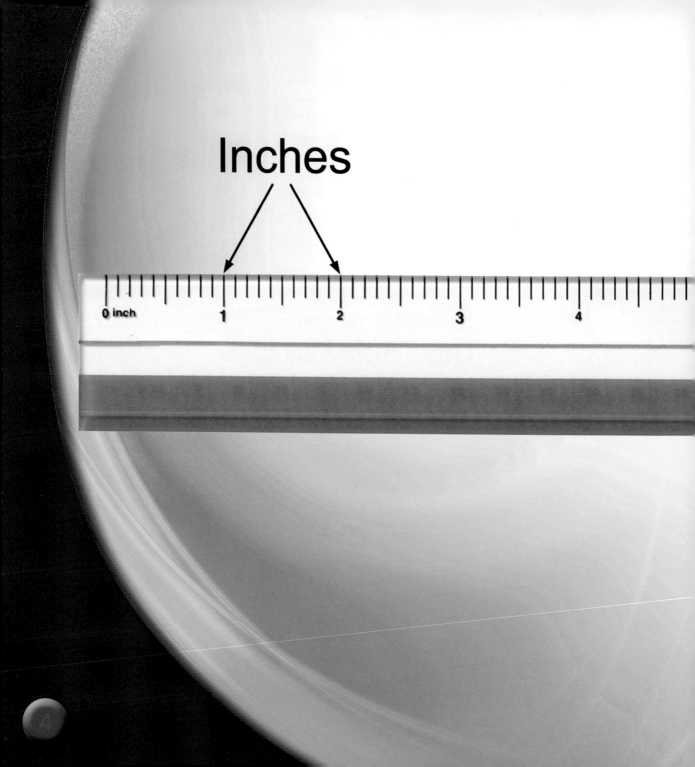

The Tools We Use

This is a **ruler**.

The ruler is marked in **inches**.

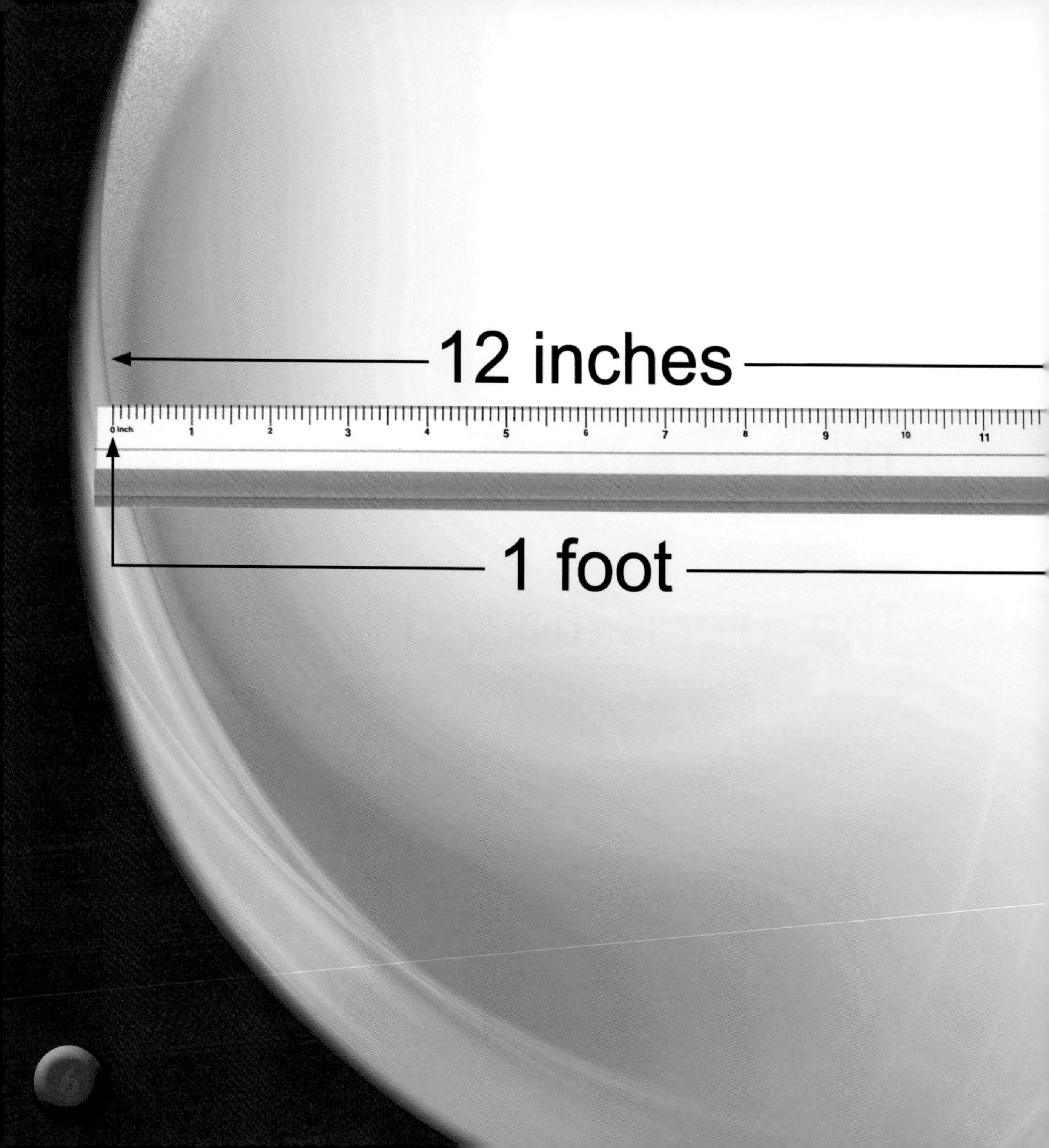
12 inches
0 inch 1 2 3 4 5 6 7 8 9 10 11
1 foot

There are 12 inches in 1 foot.

The ruler is 1 foot long.

There are 3 feet in 1 **yard**.

This tape is 12 feet long.

That is 4 yards.

How Tall?

Which cup is 3 inches tall?

Which cup is 5 inches tall?

Which bear is 10 inches tall?

Which bear is 1 foot tall?

How tall are you?

You can use a **chart** to find out.

How Wide?

Which book is 7 inches wide?

Which book is 5 inches wide?

18

Which door is wide?

Which door is not wide?

Who can use the little door?

Hold your arms out wide.

How wide are you?

Use a tape to find out!

Find Out More

BOOK

Aboff, Marcie. *If You Were an Inch or a Centimeter*. Minneapolis: Picture Window Books, 2009.

WEB SITE

NIST—Taking America's Measure: Fun Activities for Kids
www.nist.gov/public_affairs/kids/kidsmain.htm
Find games, puzzles, and information to help you learn how to measure.

Glossary

chart (CHART) a sheet of paper with lines used to measure something

inches (INCH-ez) units of measurement; there are 12 inches in 1 foot.

ruler (ROO-lur) a long flat piece of wood, metal, or plastic that is used to measure things

yard (YARD) a unit of measurement; 1 yard is equal to 3 feet.

Home and School Connection

Use this list of words from the book to help your child become a better reader. Word games and writing activities can help beginning readers reinforce literacy skills.

a	find	not	use
are	foot	out	we
arms	hold	ruler	which
bear	how	tall	who
book	in	tape	wide
can	inches	the	yard
chart	is	there	yards
cup	little	this	you
door	long	to	your
feet	marked	tools	

Index

About the Author

Cecilia Minden is the former Director of the Language and Literacy Program at the Harvard Graduate School of Education. She currently works as a literacy consultant for school and library publishers and is the author of more than 100 books for children.